A Storm Of Voices

Where Light Fractures and Nature Speaks

Jennifer Brantley Graham

BookLeaf Publishing

India | USA | UK

Dedication

To the girl who finds forever in a grain of sand,
each tiny speck a universe,
a story waiting to unfold.
This book of poetry is for you—
a tribute to your spark,
a reminder that imagination, like you,
knows no bounds.

To my late mother Ginny McElveen Graham Peele,
the most original, inventive, brilliant free spirit
(the kite to my tail)
who taught me that anything is possible
when we set our imagination free.

Preface

"Reflect" means light hits a shiny surface and bounces back at the same angle it hit it, while "refract" means light bends through a transparent surface as it enters a new medium with a different density, causing it to change direction.

In the twilight hours of morning when it is still dark and all is quiet, creativity is usually at its peak—especially when I cannot sleep. It is at this time that I am able to gain access to every thought I have compartmentalized in my mind since childhood. Long-repressed memories and ideas freely dance around in my imagination which fuels my desire to put it all into words. Through this "stream of consciousness," hidden (sometimes haunted) voices storm across paper releasing a torrential downpour of memories, dreams, and sometimes nightmares. In some poems, I become more of myself, and in others, I inhabit someone (or something) else.

"A Storm of Voices: Where Light Fractures and Nature Speaks," is a collection of narrative poems (with a few exceptions) where you, the reader, get to decide how the bending of light contributes to the meaning of each poem and whether it is Mother Nature or human nature that gives it a voice. In my experience, "Nature" provides the best platform for exploring the senses and how the presence or absence of light echoes our emotions. Some poems mirror a specific point of view (reflection), while others attempt to alter perception so the reader might interpret an idea in a different way (refraction).

Some familiar words show up in each poem. I am not one to often repeat specific words or phrases, but in this collection, they function as the bones that connect and hold it together. I have always had a love affair with language and how a certain combination of words elicits a specific sensory response.

I have reworked some old notes and ideas from past creative writing assignments from 20 plus years ago, so to a handful of readers, a couple might seem familiar. As it turns out, I stumbled across some old folders with poem and story ideas I thought had been tossed out long ago; this provided the motivation for me to revisit those thoughts and memories.

As a writer, I am always a work in progress. The most amazing aspect of poetry is that it is always open to interpretation. Whatever the case for you, I do hope you enjoy the journey. This collection presents an earnest, heartfelt stir of voices that celebrates what a mind unleashed can create in the dark.

Acknowledgements

I would like to acknowledge a handful of educators who have been a source of inspiration for all creative endeavors. Thank you to Laura Floyd, Betty Jean Godwin, Susie Hyman, Glen Gourley, Dr. Beckie Hendricks Flannagan, Phillip Gardner, Dr. Jon Tuttle, Dr. Thom Young, Dr. Jennifer Kunka, the late Dr. Edwin P. Eleazer and the late Katherine Boling for guidance and encouragement which still continue to be a huge inspiration in my pursuit of artistic expression in music, theater, and creative writing. I am eternally grateful to you all. Sometimes, one encouraging phrase is all that a potential writer needs to bloom.

Also, a huge thank you to Francis Marion University's literary journal, "The Snow Island Review" (1998-2002) for publishing some of my first attempts at poetry and fiction, a couple of which appear in this collection with some modifications.

Thank you to the late incomparable Frances Ivey Graham Player (Grandma) for all those adventures on the farm and for motivating me to become a better person with each passing day. I feel you around me always.

To my late Aunt JoBesse McElveen Waldeck, whose published books have always encouraged me to follow in her footsteps from a young age, you have motivated me more than you will ever know.

To Dean Coward, a kind, hilarious, supportive presence in my life since I was 11 years old, it is an honor to still call you friend.

If it were not for the incredible group of friends I had growing up who not only supported and encouraged me, but also participated in every play, every lip sync, every recital, every singing competition, every adventure, I would not be the person I am today or the writer I have become. I pull ideas from so many great memories shared with you all: Shannon, Dean, Sheila, Susan, Amy, Darlene, Drew, Dee, Shelley, and the late Kellie--I could not have asked for better company.

Also, if it were not for Emily Dickinson, I never would have tried to write poetry in the first place. Flannery O'Connor's short stories and the works of Edgar Allen Poe ignited my desire to put pen to paper when I wrote my first poem "The Terror Within" at 15 years old.

Foul Weather

I lie awake—restless,
nestled in my canopy bed,
its lacy fringes above me
waving like eyelashes.
I cling to the plush beagle
cradled under my chin;
mud-stained and worn,
stuffing weeps through its skin.
Sleep won't come.

Scared by the storm outside
—a black horse—
charging, impatiently
into my sunflower room.
My skin beads sweat,
bed sheets stick like tar;
tangled so, they constrict me.
I grasp my beagle's tattered ear,
its body dangling from my hand.

I run, stumble down the hall.
Hair, like spiderwebs
glues itself to eyelids;
skin pulls taught around bone,
turning color pale.
A million dancing flies
dart backward—
churning, fluttering,
tickling flesh like ice.

The beagle's ear
still clutched in my hand,
its limp body now
lying at my feet—
torn threads exposing a wound.
I pick it up—cradle it gently,
see the kitchen light streak
through the dun-colored paneling—
a door cracked open just enough.

Daddy delivers tormenting blows.
Outside the storm grows
wild and furious.
Rain pounds liquid fists
into the roof.
Thunder rumbles,
shakes the floorboards.

Words howl and crash;
his temper rages.
Winds screech nails across glass.

Mamma sits wilted,
like crumpled over newspaper.
Lightning flashes a crooked grin
through a trembling window.
Wet makeup muddies cheeks—
whimpers jolt forth frantic breaths.
I bolt out—
scurry back to my canopy bed.
I stuff a tissue into my beagle's naked sore.
Rain still pulses outside my window.

I climb under sheets—
pull covers tightly overhead.
Tree shadows yawn
and stretch around me,
bruising walls.
Eyelids tug shut.
Slowly, my sunflower room fades.
Sleep chews then swallows,
savoring each bite.

Jack

Because of you—I sit,
a dismembered oak,
hunched over
in a sudden freeze.

How quickly snow
strips limbs bare,
raw pulp exposed,
withered roots anchored.

Deep fists clenched
in a silent scream.

You—Wild Drifter,
masked behind sallow,
crystalline eyes,
bringing icicle daggers
that bite deep.

I—haunted vessel,

a twisted bleeding space,
tear snow-flaked crimson cheeks
in an isolated whiteness
bruised blue.

Because of you, I shiver,
a blanketed heap of naked bone:

Everything winter-stifled
love-swallowed,
blizzard-kissed, numb.
Folding into myself, I quit you.

Killed quietly.

The Embalmer

Cobalt streams through diaphanous silk threads.

Spittle glistens, loops, tangles winged victims.

Sinister wizard, Osirian wonder,

A black stilted shadow—venomed needles.

Fangs prey on bug flesh, the whir of wings clipped.

Mummified moth—helpless siren clouded.

Darkness spins, weaving mesh around slow death.

Visceral matter consumed—a cocoon film stills.

The web cradles a new jeweled token,

one less innocent drawn to the moon's light.

On Imagination

Welcome the never-ceasing brain rain
falling about the place.
Storms of ideas
pouring into space.
Soaring through time,
gathering all without a trace—
Adored with sponge-like affection.
Cherished at once,
then matched to a face.

Here, thoughts stir awake,
a flickering candle flame,
each voice a cry,
waltzing through cracks in the mind—
old memories spill out,
a rushing river after rain.
Shapes seem familiar,
yet shimmering and new.

Words emerge like fireflies,

each glowing with charge,
filling the pages
with light that fractures,
a million shards sparkling
under the touch of ideas.

Here, the mind is a bustling cafe,
where dreams collide and mingle,
each thought multiplying,
stars unearthing darkness,
pulling me into their cosmic rhythm.

In these stolen hours,
I find clarity,
pen in hand,
as sight becomes sound,
and echoes of the night wrap
around speech—
words birthed from dark corners,
secrets set free
in evening's embrace.

Finding Vincent

The starry sky swirls above—
a night captured in brushstrokes,
now interwoven into cell phones,
the glow of wallpaper casting shadows.

But I thrive still,
hair tousled like harvest fields,
eyes alive with desperation,
clutching a palette not of paint,
but of feelings,
shouting colors at every turn.

Each year that undulates past
brings new sounds, new stories—
blue and indigo linger,
capture life
not as it is, but as it should be.

Beneath the weight of night traffic
and the glare of streetlights,

beauty dances,
wanders in moonlit alley ways
as spirals of stars
descend to earth
and Van Gogh smiles.

A Sparkle in Flight

In the hush of twilight,
they emerge,
tiny lanterns flickering,
each a whispered secret
of the summer night.

They dance a soft sonnet,
a symphony of light and shadow,
painting air with luminescent dreams—
majestic choreography
beneath the vast, night sky.

Children chase them,
hands outstretched,
laughter spilling out like stardust,
treasuring the glow,
each flitter a fleeting wish,
held tightly in hand
with innocent wonder.

Bright orbs weave through trees,
constellations brought to earth
in the ephemeral,
fragile iridescence,
that brightens then fades,
yet lingers in memory
long after night has surrendered
to morning.

Oh, to be a firefly,
caught in the gentle embrace
of the evening,
a pulsating beacon of hope,
illuminating darkness—
a moment of reflection
in a world that often forgets
to look up.

Southern Pine

In the shadow of night
where cricket-song
ornaments the air,
flesh cradles stories,
worn like the edges
of forgotten pages.

Bone-splintered skin,
a gnarled tapestry
of scars and reverence
rooted deep beneath the foliage—
solid—holding upright.

Each fissure tells a tale
of battles fought in the dark,
a life that bloomed then withered
beneath the caress
of Nature's fingers.

Wearing skin like armor

with all its jagged edges—
splintered bark,
the moon lighting on the lips of limbs,
branches outstretched—
grasp and swallow star-shine.

A lasting testament to the journey.
Each ridge a chapter,
each ring a poem,
woven into the wilderness
of all that is me.

Piano Lesson

In a quiet room,
shrouded in silence,
I am 88 keys,
black and white bones
upright—centuries old.
Waiting, silent
for the spark
of some erotic finger.
I am much more
than wood and wire.

1st Movement

Once a kingdom of sound,
wood cradling melodies
dancing through time,
stories of love, loss,
and fleeting moments,
hushed now
by the weight of longing.

Where is the musician
who translates the language.
crescendo, diminuendo,
the sweet ache of chords.
Mozart's touch glides
—glisando—
Beethoven's hand pulses
—sforzando—
Will the melody ever find
its way home?

Each key stroke
a thundering tone,
full of expression,
vibrations chasing echoes
off walls, through air,
souls bursting open,
sound pulsing
with every twist of emotion.

In this sanctuary,
every strike is a choice,
a risk and a promise—to reach out
and awaken stories
from slumber.

Linger a moment longer,
in the hush before creation.
A single touch will set me free—
let the music rise,
to highlight the room
with the fire
of forgotten dreams.

2nd Movement

I sit in a room,
more than mahogany
and hammers,
keys resting,
where every strike—
a breath, a moment,
pulses.

Dust drapes my frame,
the secrets of songs
long forgotten
wait for touch,
a hand ready—
elegant and sure,
coaxing forth magic,
bathing the space
in sound like sunshine.

Fingers dancing,
black then white, the drum of rhythm.
Concertos, symphonies, sonatas
reverberating through some
distant reverie.

Keys sing out,
joy pulling the room alive
like the tide meeting shore.
Where silence lingers too long,
the echo of sound
sinks deep into bones,
and shadows hold still—

Here lies a promise,
a sitting invitation to leap,
to float on chords,
and rise above the stillness,
while the melody weaves a tapestry,
multiple threads of light,
glimmering in the afternoon.

Where music waltzes in
and tastes the air
until every bone dances free,
and every note resounds—

a story waiting to unfold: a breath,
a moment, a memory.

In a quiet room,
shrouded in silence,
I am 88 keys,
black and white bones
upright—centuries old.
Waiting, silent
for the spark
of some erotic finger.
I am much more
than wood and wire.

Childhood Reverie

I miss the girl—
skipping stones across the pond,
giggling like the wind,
carefree as drifting clouds,
dreams unfurling like paper airplanes,
soaring high on the breath of summer.

In the golden light of morning,
she stands by the old wooden fence,
where the sun spills over fields,
barefoot on warm earth,
chasing butterflies
spinning in circles,
the world a blur of blue and green.

The old barn door creaks and sighs,
revealing a hayloft full of secrets,
fantasies stitched together
with laughter and dust
in the scent of earth after rain—

captured in time.

She sees her favorite tree,
its branches a kingdom
where she ruled as queen,
a crown of daisies in her hair,
and the blissfully endless sky
her castle full of daydreams.

In twilight moments,
I catch a glimpse—
the girl with wild eyes
who whispered secrets to the stars.
Her paintbrush at the ready,
the world an empty canvas.

Now, I wear the gravity of choices
with the quiet ache of time,
tracing fingers over flesh,
wondering if she still dances
beneath the skin of my memories.

Days are packed tight,
with schedules and screens,
the girl buried beneath the weight
of what I must do.
Yet I hold her close,

a shimmer of light
in a universe that spins
entirely too fast.

To Schizophrenia

I.

In the mirror, a parade of faces.
each one winks, some frown,
a few dance like they own the room.
So here I am,
a circus of selves,
a juggler tossing words into air,
each a little quirky, a little mad.

I tip my hat to the crowd,
welcome them to the stage.
This is my truth,
a comedy of errors.
In this wild universe,
who needs just one—
when you can be everyone
and no one all at once.

II.
In the quiet corners of my mind
voices dance
and dash like thunder—
Friend or foe?
I wade through a foggy sea
where reality bends
and speaks in riddles.

Sometimes, I am a queen,
crowned by chaos—
other times, a ghost
lost in the hallways.

III.
In cluttered spaces,
thoughts collide,
shadows skip in darkness.
Multiple voices
shriek and giggle,
unwavering and fragile,
to walk on edge.

An artist crafting worlds,

bits and pieces
break like glass underfoot.
The sky ripples in rainbows
that only I can see.
Memories slip through fingers,
grains of sand,
too quick to hold.

The room spins—
a choir of strangers
that never sleep,
hidden truths unravel
behind walls,
once locked away.

On-lookers pass judgment,
never understanding
the weight of the sky we carry
or the storms that rage
beneath skin's surface.

'POE' session

By the dim light
of a candle's flicker
I carve words
from the marrow of night,
inking a potion
exotic and rich,
spinning webs
of melancholy and madness,
each stanza a steady pulse—
pounding onto paper.

The clock ticks louder,
thumping in the dead silence.
Secret eyes lurk with interest
from dark corners
where dust gathers.

Is it the wind playing tricks
or the remnants of nightmares
spilling into the waking mind,

blurring lines,
the known and unknown,
where the mundane
becomes extraordinary.

Things stir: a rustle, a creak,
a door left ajar.
Footsteps echo
though no feet tread.
Imagination runs wild—
reason flees
like a startled rabbit.

In the quiet chaos,
there is a strange comfort
in bumps and rustles—
the intangible presence—
a reminder you are alive
and part of the wild night
where mystery dwells
and the heart pulses
quickest in the dark.

Catching the Train

In the storm, I stand
on the railroad tracks,
a silhouette in the tumult,
wearing a nightgown,
billowing like the ghosts
of bedtime stories—
waiting to surrender.

Thunder grumbles,
the heartbeat a constant reminder
of all the dreams that slipped
through my fingers
like the fading daylight.

Tracks stretch ahead,
steel veins of life rushing by,
lingering in the grip of a moment,
the weight of memories
heavy as storm clouds.

Lightning fractures the sky
illuminating a tear-streaked face,
a fleeting glimpse of vulnerability
that clings like dampness—
a chill that wraps around me
like the nightgown's frayed edges.

I have always listened
to the rumble of trains,
the promise of escape—
but the tracks are cold
underneath my feet.
The earth beneath the storm feels
more familiar than the places
I dream of running to.

I am waiting for the train
to round the curve ahead,
close enough
to catapult the rocks
across the tracks like popcorn.
Then, I will lie down,
close my eyes and sleep.

Dancing Pig

Under the bright spotlights, I stand,
in pig ears and a curly tail,
soft swirls of tulle catching giggles,
fingers twirling satin edges—
music begins to play.

A sea of glittery girls stretch and sway,
legs long like afternoon shadows,
polished glass smiles shining.
I stand backstage,
a timid bloom in a garden of stars.

Why do they look like sunlight?
Voices curl in my mind,
heart slamming against walls,
loud and heavy, like bright satin
that squeezes my waist,
hugging skin too tight.

In moments of pirouettes and leaps,

feet stumble, clumsy on the stage,
Happiness battling truth—
teaching something new.
A mirror reflects more than a face.

The room pulses with an odd silence,
darkness hides behind shimmering eyes,
A strangeness washes over—
For the first time, the divide
between what is beautiful and what is broken
swallows everything.

In this fleeting moment, colors bleed,
music lifts spirits higher.
Climbing out of darkness,
feet pound the floor in rhythm.
The mirror tells only one story,
but I now know the others.

Each twirl, each step, a reminder of worth,
resilience wrapped in pink and joy,
The weight of awareness says
I don't need tan skin or long legs
to sparkle.

With every twist, every turn,
dancing on dreams, not just applause,

laughter bubbles up
blush as cotton candy.

I grin, arms like wings outstretched,
filling the stage with a different light—
Not the gleam of a perfect girl,
but the glow of a fat kid
who dares to dance,
flaunting her pink tutu.

Echoes of Emily

Anger

I.

Anger is a quiet storm,
rising like a tide,
that shatters corners,
where silence rattles—
a soft rebellion,
gathering strength.

It boils beneath skin,
a glimmer of heat,
igniting thoughts,
sharp as broken glass,
cutting through the calm,
leaving only echoes.

Where does it go,
this fire that shimmers—
the heart a prisoner,

hands clenched tight?
Flowers wilt in its wake,
and laughter feels foreign.

But sometimes,
when the storm has passed,
a quiet sigh escapes,
and in the stillness,
I ponder its shape—
a lesson wrapped in rage,
a brush with truth,
reminding us we are alive.

II.
A spark that flutters
in the chest,
a storm cloud brewing,
untamed and wild,
hiding in shadows,
a lightning strike.

It curls fingers,
tight around the heart,
pushing thoughts
—angry waves—
against the shore of reason,
where calm waters go to die.

Silent thunder rolls--
the face sometimes
full of boiling tears
and sharp-edged smirks,
as if every expression
were a dagger
poised to puncture.

In the aftermath,
Sifting through the wreckage,
I find pieces to mend,
realizing there's more to be
than fire and rage.

Desire

I.
In shadows lean, a glance held tight,
Words curl like smoke.
Fingers brush—electric,
—a silent pulse—
A dance beneath soft sheets,
Where breaths collide—
A moth to open flame.
A hunger, naked and raw, ripples.

Time, a thief, swiftly plucks
The moment—but oh,
A heart's hunger,
Burns brighter in the dark.

II.
In shadows deep, a yearning glow,
A spark, unseen, ignites the night,
A passion billowing—it knows—
A tremor, soft, a quiet fight.
Petals quiver on the breeze.
Dancing flames, yet kept at bay,
Desire's breath a teasing tease,
The moments slip, then fade away.

No chains to bind, yet stronger still,
A fleeting glance, a knowing sigh,
In silent rooms, this aching thrill—
A secret wish that dares to fly.

Gone Boy Blues

The boy that got away,
like a sock in the dryer,
lost to the abyss of mismatched laundry—
who knew he would escape
while I was busy folding my heart?

He had a smile,
a dazzling masterpiece
like Picasso in a thrift store—
quirky, confusing,
and a tad overpriced.
I could never refuse such charm.

He'd pop in
like a bubble in my soda,
effervescent and fleeting.
I'd sip the fizz,
thinking he'd stick around.
But he floated away,
leaving the flat taste of absence behind.

I'm now left here,
a collection of "what-if's"
like dusty trophies of missed chances,
with a heart that's grown much too sarcastic,
a comedian at an empty mic.

So this is for you
the boy that got away—
may you find your fortune
in the land of lost socks and bad jokes
while I continue to master
the art of being alone.

Undead on Vacation

Dracula at the beach,
squinting at sunlight,
eyes shrouded in dark shades,
hiding from bright rays—

Sunblock slathered on thick,
a stark white mask—
no SPF high enough
to save me from the day.

A black cape flutters
in the breeze,
caught somewhere
between goth and goofball,
trying hard to fit in.

Silly kids build castles—
sandy and giddy,
splashing in the surf,
the sand between my toes.

I throw a frisbee.
It flops forward
like a dead bat on shore.
I play it uber cool,
fanging a hotdog
with ketchup.

Seagulls squawk and wail,
dive-bombing my towel.
Flashing a grin that could horrify
the bravest of sunbathers,
I hiss—
gulp one down (feathers and all)
with lightning speed.

I'm an out-of-place movie star,
a vision sitting
in an unearthed casket.
As the sun sinks into the sea,
eyes glare across sand
as if lit from within.

At dusk, nobody notices
I am the only one
drinking cherry juice
with a frown.

I-20 Standstill

In the thick of rush hour,
horns blare like angry geese,
I grip the wheel, a ship at sea,
waves of brake lights crashing behind.

To my left, a clown in a little green coupe,
wiggling his fingers from the window,
I squint, *is that a wave or a warning?*
Maybe he just forgot he had to drive.

The light turns green, but we're paused
as if the world took a coffee break—
I wave a peace sign—or a car initiation—
either way, this is my chance.

Behind me, a minivan with a disco ball
makes me chuckle, envisioning a dance-off,
a traffic jam twist—tires squealing,
all car doors flying open like a breeze.

And in my mirror, Mrs. Johnson,
the queen of the cul-de-sac,
teeth glaring daggers,
covered in breakfast biscuit crumbs
(can't be too fierce with crumbs like that).

I wave, both brake lights staccato
to the rhythm of this symphony.
Road rage disappears.
It's just me, the clown, and Mrs. Johnson
dancing in traffic.

Behind the wheel, we're all just human,
steering aluminum cans through life—
frustration turned to laughter,
pouring out like sunshine,
rescuing those usually too angry to care.

A Battle of Clicks

I. Round One

In the parking lot,
I hold plastic in my hand,
cool and familiar;
it's not the key but
the remote for a world
where laughter flows,
and faces flicker on a screen,
not a car door waiting
for the familiar click.

I press the button,
fingers dancing on habit,
a wishful spark in my brain,
my mind a wild carousel
spinning out of control,
everything feels jumbled,
like a puzzle left unsolved.

A moment of silence,
then a soft beep,
the stillness of the lot
brimming with hope—
but it's not my ride
that answers my call,
just the chill of the evening air
that wraps around me
like a blanket.

Reality rolls in,
and I drop the faux-key,
unbelievably amused,
at this little mix-up.
It's just a fleeting distraction,
a reminder to pause,
to breathe, to ground myself
in a world bursting with noise.

With a laugh, I reach for the right one,
feeling the weight of metal,
I unlock myself
from these tangled thoughts,
climb in, and take a moment,
to just sit in the stillness,
before hitting the road again.

II. Round Two

In the glow of dusk, I wander,
my mind a wild kite,
tethered by restless thoughts,
chasing ideas down the hall.

I reach for comfort,
the flicker of the screen,
but my car key fob
is in my hands,
shiny and cold.

A click, a press,
my heart beats in time
with a small red light,
but the world stays silent.
No scenes to greet me,
just the echo
of my own bewildered thoughts.

I sit here, puzzled,
the moon peering through the window,
while outside, engines roar,
and people move in patterns.

But here, just me,
holding my keys like magic wands,
seeking solace
in a world gone hazy.

One last effort,
one last click,
then laughter spills out,
a mix of disbelief and joy,
as I step back,
to gather the pieces
of my scattered mind.

Strange how moments drift,
how the ordinary twists
in the chaos of daily life,
where sometimes,
a car key fob
is just a bridge,
between what is real,
and what I think I need.

III. Round Three

In the glow of the evening,
thoughts tangled like old earphones,

I reach for my key fob,
hand grazing over silence,
searching for what I need,
but my mind is drifting,
like leaves on a restless breeze.

I click, expecting a door to open,
but only the TV hums back,
a flicker on the screen,
as if it knows my scramble,
my weariness woven deep
in the fabric of this day.

Remote in hand,
I fumble with buttons—
a chosen movie turns to snow,
and all I can feel is lost,
a traveler without a map,
a sailor unmoored at dusk.

So I drop the fob and the remote,
let them lay where they fall,
and sighing, I give up,
the world slows down
with each step to my room,
where blankets wrap around me,
a soft retreat from the chaos.

Morning can find its way,
but tonight is for surrender,
each breath a gentle promise—
tomorrow, perhaps,
I'll locate the keys and the remote—
for now, sleep sings
and all is well in the dark.

Out of Time

I. Chase

In the corners of night,
where echoes crawl like spiders,
eyes close, begging for release
and find darkness calling.

Shadows twist and reach,
clutching at my throat.
Fear ripples in waves,
walls breathe a heavy sigh
as the clock ticks loudly,
the only sound in this hollow space.

Faces—familiar, yet strange—
watch from the edge of sleep,
their eyes dim and hollow,
mouths moving silently,
spitting words I dare not hear.

I run through murky fog,
legs trapped in heavy chains,
fingers reaching for light,
but shadows dance away,
leading me deeper
into the maze of my own mind.

A scream lodged tight in my chest,
rubbed raw against the dark,
as I wake gasping,
drenched in fear,
bathed in sweat,
the night still snarling outside.

But morning comes,
soft and calm,
washing away nightmares
with the promise of another day,
but I hold the darkness close,
like a secret between friends,
waiting patiently for its return.

II. Trap

In the stillness of sleep,
shadows creep in,

familiar faces twist
into fearful shapes,
a whisper at the edge of thought,
where secrets come to dance.

A heavy weight sits on the chest,
the walls close in,
and breath becomes shallow,
each heartbeat a drum,
a promise of impending doom,
the flurry of thoughts
that chase and claw.

Running through a maze of doors,
echoes of laughter fading—
ghosts trying to hold me tight,
except it's not a hug,
it's a grasp, harsh and cold.

I scream, but sound holds its breath,
trapped inside a noisy cage,
as the world spins,
defying the laws of light and trust,
dreams should be safe
yet they turn and twist.

And in the thick of it,

a glimmer of hope
that dawn will break,
banishing the night,
where shadows no longer chase,
and silent shrieks
become quiet memories,
fading away when light returns.

III. Release

In the silence of the night,
spirits wander,
whispers caught in wind,
drifting through rows of stone towers,
standing watch over secrets long buried.

Moonlight stains faces,
soft shadows on forgotten names,
where ivy winds like old stories
and moss cradles the weight of time.
A quiet chorus,
echoes rise from earth,
haunting memories
pulled from slumber.

They glide past weathered angels,
wings heavy with tales
carrying laughter and sighs,
dreams lost to the past,
pale figures with eyes like stars,
searching for the living,
flitting between earth and sky.

Each invisible step a life lived,
of love and loss bound in night
roaming through memories.
Laughter mingles
with the rustle of leaves
an eternal dance upon the grave.

Hold tightly to warmth,
each living heartbeat.
Time twines around us
like a foggy mist
while ghosts still roam free.

Spinning Darkness

In the hush of fading light,
shadows stretch fingers wide—
murmurs softly weave through air,
a gentle pull, a heavy sigh.

Death, a quiet visitor,
strolling through evening mist,
wraps the world in monotone gray,
each heartbeat, a final twist.

Darkness holding fast,
like the night, it knows no shame—
a breath, a pulse, then worlds depart,
unraveled threads, the same.

Yet in this stark and veiled charade,
we look for stars that glimmer, glow—
a promise that beyond the deep,
somewhere, somehow, we still grow.

In shadows creeping, quiet and thin,
Death whispers soft, to gentle kin.
Darkness grins, a fading light,
A shroud of peace, upon the night.

No need for fear, no need for sound,
In silence deep, we touch the ground.
Life's bright spark, a fleeting guest,
In darkness born, we find our rest.

The Bending of Light

Light bends and breaks,
dancing through glass—
refraction, a twist in direction,
shows a world we cannot see.

Colors shift, truths unfold,
a poet spinning words,
shaping abstract ideas
into vibrant beams.

But there's also reflection,
a simple glance in the mirror,
truth staring back,
an image caught, unchanged.

The poet's words, a surface,
a stir of voices,
all cradled tight, set in motion,
a winding river holding the sky.

A poet bends or breaks,
a tree in strong winds,
churning out verse
to pull in light, or hold it still—
A world refracted,
or a face reflected,
the voice of shared humanity.